EVERYDAY STOIC RESILIENCE

EVERYDAY STOIC RESILIENCE

INSPIRATIONAL QUOTES AND DAILY PROMPTS TO BUILD AN UNSHAKAKBLE MINDSET

Published and distributed by:

SOUND WISDOM
P.O. Box 310
Shippensburg, PA 17257-0310

717-530-2122

info@soundwisdom.com

www.soundwisdom.com

ISBN 13 TP: 978-1-64095-744-2

ISBN 13 eBook: 978-1-64095-745-9

For Worldwide Distribution, Printed in the U.S.A.

1 2 3 4 5 6 7 8 / 30 29 28 27 26

CONTENTS

INTRODUCTION

The philosophy of Stoicism was originally put forward by its founder, Zeno, in about 300 BCE. It was then systematized by Chrysippus in the 200s. But the true shape of Stoicism was formed in the writings of three later men: Marcus Aurelius, Seneca, and Epictetus. Their writings expounded the Stoic philosophy, and they also transmitted it to later generations. Each played a crucial yet unique role.

The earliest writer was Seneca (about 4 BCE to 65 CE). He was a statesman, dramatist, and advisor to Emperor Nero who adapted Greek Stoic philosophy to the realities of Roman political life. In many ways, he popularized the philosophy into a true movement.

Seneca's primary focus was on managing emotions, especially anger and tranquility. He wrote letters and essays on how to live virtuously in a politically corrupt and dangerous world. His writings heavily influenced later Christian and Renaissance thinkers.

Following Seneca was Epictetus (approximately 50 to 135 CE). Epictetus was a unique voice among Stoics, having been born into slavery and later freed. He also did not write his own books; his disciple, Arrian, recorded his verbal teachings for posterity.

Epictetus was a practical Stoic who focused heavily on personal discipline and responsibility. His keynote was the now-famous Stoic dichotomy of control: Some things are up to us; others are not. Speaking as a former slave, he provided deep insights into finding inner freedom, regardless of external conditions.

Finally, the emperor Marcus Aurelius (121 to 180 CE) gave us a record of Stoicism in action from a position of the highest authority. He emphasized humility, rationality, and acceptance of fate—an interesting focal point for a person in such a high position of power.

Aurelius made his life a model of his philosophy, living out the principles he espoused despite the heavy pressures of leadership. He kept a personal journal, the *Meditations*, in which he reflected deeply on mortality, duty, resilience, and service. He truly became the symbolic embodiment of the "philosopher king."

In his daily life, he repeatedly dealt with critical issues; in his *Meditations*, he repeatedly zooms out and looks at the big picture above it all. For Aurelius, human life is brief, fame is fleeting, and all things return to Nature.

The emperor often reminds himself to humbly do his duty, accepting things that are outside of his control—which was the core element that Epictetus focused on. For Epictetus, each person is in control of their own judgments, desires, and actions. But no one is in control of their own health, reputation, wealth, or the choices of others. For him, suffering comes from trying to take control of things that are not ours to control.

Epictetus tends to use a sharp tone, as a demanding teacher. His Stoicism is not for personal comfort, but for developing the highest moral character. Fittingly, the former slave has deep insights into how a slave can be free if his mind is free, while an emperor can be enslaved by his passions.

Seneca also takes a hard look at the passions. He emphasizes managing emotion within real life—regulating it, but not suppressing it. His views on emotions are the most nuanced of the three, and his tone is more caring.

The Stoic life is very much a journey, for Seneca. He admits of his own imperfections and sees the Stoic life as a path of continual improvement—not a simple and immediate key to sagehood. Many times, he exhorts those who have fallen short simply to begin again, make another try, and not get so discouraged that they give up. Being on the path is progress. Leaving it would be the only true failure.

All three of these writers share the core Stoic beliefs that virtue is the only true good, external events are not inherently good or bad, and reason should guide life. However, each has his own personal focus.

Epictetus asks, "What is in my control right now?"

Seneca asks, "How should I handle human weakness?"

Marcus Aurelius asks, "How do I live rightly within the vast universe?"

These three figures together represent the heart of Roman Stoicism. They preserved the philosophy originally developed by the Greeks, and each, in his own way, turned the abstract logic of Stoicism into practical, daily realities.

In this 90-day reflection journal, you will find quotes from these three great Stoics. The topics covered are some of the core principles of Stoicism, with each writer providing his own unique angle on the idea. Through reflection questions and several larger exercises, you will be encouraged to take a close look at your own life, and to interact deeply with the philosophy. Let these ancient philosophers speak into your daily life today, guiding you into a more resilient Stoic outlook for your future.

CONTROL

Things in my life right now that bother me, worry me, or upset me:

Things in my life right now that I am happy, satisfied, and content with:

1

Of things, some are in our power, and others are not. In our power are opinion, movement toward a thing, desire, aversion, turning from a thing; and in a word, *whatever are our acts*. Not in our power are the body, property, reputation, official power, and in a word, *whatever are not our own acts.* And the things in our power are by nature free, not subject to restraint or hindrance; but the things not in our power are weak, slavish, subject to restraint, in the power of others.

—Epictetus,
The Enchiridion, I

REFLECT

From my lists, which items fall under "my actions"? According to Epictetus' definition, include anything that is a type of "opinion"—thoughts, preferences, feelings about anything:

Which items are not "my actions"? Who has power over these things, if not me?

2

You may fetter my leg, but my will not even Zeus himself can overpower.

—Epictetus, *The Discourses*,
"Things Which Are in Our Power
and Not in Our Power"

REFLECT

One thing from my list of worries that is not within my power:

Why am I worried about this?

Looking at my list of things that make me happy, am I deriving my satisfaction mostly from things that are within my control or from things that are not?

What would happen to my mental or emotional state if something outside of my control took one of these things away?

3

Certainly, death and life, honor and dishonor, pain and pleasure—all these things equally happen to good people and bad, and they are things which make us neither better nor worse. Therefore they are neither good nor evil.

—The *Meditations* of Marcus Aurelius,
Book II: xi

REFLECT

My ideal life:

Where is the pain, conflict with people, or eventual death in this picture? Have I been striving for an impossibly perfect life?

4

If you are pained by any external thing, it is not this thing that disturbs you, but your own judgment about it. And it is in your power to wipe out this judgment now.

—The *Meditations* of Marcus Aurelius,
Book VIII: xlvii

REFLECT

In what ways have I made pleasure or the good opinion of others into the "good" that I seek in life—or how have I made pain or the disapproval of people into a "bad" thing I need to avoid?

____

____

____

____

____

____

If I change my opinion about "good" and "bad" and only concern myself with thing things that are within my control, which sources of worry from my list will I be removing from my life?

____

____

____

____

____

____

5

"I may become a poor man!"

I shall then be one among many.

"I may be exiled!"

I shall then regard myself as born in the place to which I shall be sent.

"They may put me in chains!"

What then? Am I free from bonds now? Behold this clogging burden of a body, to which nature has fettered me!

"I shall die!" you say.

You mean to say, "I shall cease to run the risk of sickness; I shall cease to run the risk of imprisonment; I shall cease to run the risk of death."

—Seneca, *Letter XXV*: "On Reformation"

REFLECT

Looking at my list of worries, are any of these unique to me? Who else struggles with these problems? Do I know people who have it worse than I do?

If I take one item from my list of worries and reframe my perspective to consider this a normal part of life, how does that change its influence on my mental or emotional health?

6

Everywhere and at all times it is in your power piously to acquiesce in your present condition, and to behave justly to those who are about you, and to exert your skill upon your present thoughts, that nothing will steal into them without being well examined.

—The *Meditations* of Marcus Aurelius,
Book VII: liv

REFLECT

How do I feel about the idea of accepting an unpleasant situation—even if it is something that genuinely cannot be changed?

What cultural or personal experiences have shaped my outlook on the acceptance of something I don't like?

7

Unless I think that what has happened is an evil, I am not injured. And it is in my power not to think so.

—The *Meditations* of Marcus Aurelius, Book VII: xiv

REFLECT

An experience that upset me deeply, but which seemed like no big deal to someone else:

Were they completely off base and insensitive about this? If not, why did this issue seem like no problem to them? Is there some way I can use that outside perspective to shift my own point of view on my problems?

8

Begin the morning by saying to yourself, "I shall meet with the busybody, the ungrateful, arrogant, deceitful, envious, unsocial. They are that way because of their ignorance of good and evil. But I who have seen the nature of the good, that it is beautiful, and of the bad, that it is ugly, and the nature of him who does wrong, that it is akin to me—I can neither be injured by any of them, for no one can put upon me what is ugly, nor can I be angry with others nor hate them."

—The *Meditations* of Marcus Aurelius,
Book II: i

REFLECT

A few times when people (*not* intimate or close personal connections) hurt, wounded, offended, or upset me because I expected something different (or better) from them:

Why did I think that these people should behave better than this? Would I have felt differently about their actions or words if I had expected the worst from them?

9

Remember that it is not the one who reviles you or strikes you who insults you, but it is your opinion about these things as being insulting. When then a person irritates you, you must know that it is your own opinion which has irritated you.

—Epictetus, *The Enchiridion*, XX

REFLECT

Five insults or offenses people have given me:

1. ______________________________
2. ______________________________
3. ______________________________
4. ______________________________
5. ______________________________

Consequences of each offense, *excluding* my feelings (i.e., actual physical results of what they did or said):

1. ______________________________
2. ______________________________
3. ______________________________
4. ______________________________
5. ______________________________

Did any of these consequences affect "things within my control"—that is, my own actions? What would be the most Stoic way of looking at these experiences?

10

Consider that people will do the same things anyway, even though you should burst.

—The *Meditations* of Marcus Aurelius,
Book VIII: iv

REFLECT

The most frustrating person in my life (and why):

Have I been trying to change this person, even if I only do so in my mind or heart? Have I been *wanting* them to be someone they are not, and getting upset when they fail to change?

Since this person's actions are clearly not within my control, what can I start doing today to shift my perspective on them?

RETHINKING MY LISTS

Go back to the two lists you made at the beginning of this section and organize these aspects of your life into the following chart:

Things I can control:	Things outside of my control:

REFLECT

How are your sources of satisfaction or worry distributed? What might need to change, here?

TIME

HOW I SPEND MY WEEK

Fill out the following weekly planner with your average activities on each day, for each hour. Don't worry too much about little specifics or weekly variations. Just in general, get a picture of what you do with your time each week:

TIME	MONDAY	TUESDAY	WEDNESDAY	THURSDAY	FRIDAY	SATURDAY
12:00 AM						
1:00 AM						
2:00 AM						
3:00AM						
4:00 AM						
5:00 AM						
6:00 AM						
7:00 AM						
9:00 AM						
10:00 AM						
11:00 AM						
12:00 PM						
1:00 PM						
2:00 PM						
3:00 PM						
4:00 PM						
5:00 PM						
6:00 PM						
7:00 PM						
9:00 PM						
10:00 PM						
11:00 PM						

Now re-examine your boxes. For example, if you have blocked out an 8-hour day for "work," how much of your time at work do you spend on your phone? What little activities might also be missing from this picture—things that fill up only a few minutes, not a whole hour, but that you still spend time on, weekly?

11

Men covetously guard their property, but when it comes to their time, they are most wasteful. People live as though they would live forever.

—Seneca, *On the Shortness of Life*, III

REFLECT

Where have I been allowing people to steal my time—on special occasions, or possibly on a weekly basis?

If that time were, instead, an amount of money or a valuable piece of property, would I allow it to be stolen? What would I do to protect it?

12

Since it is possible that you may depart from life this very moment, regulate every act and thought accordingly. Every person's life is sufficient.

—The *Meditations* of Marcus Aurelius,
Book II: vi, xi

REFLECT

If I had an extra hour on my weekly schedule, what's the number-one thing I want to put in that spot?

If it's true that "every person's life is sufficient," what might I be able to do to *make* room in my schedule for this number-one thing?

13

We do not receive a short life, but we make it a short one; and we are not poor in days, but wasteful of them.

—Seneca, *On the Shortness of Life*, I

REFLECT

Things I feel like I never have enough time for:

____

____

____

If I knew I only had 10 years left to live, my top priorities would be:

____

____

____

____

Things that I would remove completely from my weekly schedule:

____

____

____

____

14

A person cannot lose either the past or the future—for what you do not have, how can anyone take this from you? If it is true that the present is the only thing which you have, and that you cannot lose a thing you do not have, the present is the only thing of which you can be deprived.

—The *Meditations* of Marcus Aurelius,
Book II: xiv

REFLECT

Do I use my time as though I realize that the future is not actually in my possession? What do I do with my time that assumes I have a long future guaranteed to me?

Since all I have is the present, what is the one thing I can do today that will make me satisfied when reflecting on my day?

15

Consider that the times of opportunity are perishing. If you only fall a-nodding a little, all that you have up to this time collected is gone.

—Epictetus, *The Discourses*, "What Things We Should Exchange for Other Things"

REFLECT

A time when I had made a lot of progress toward something, but I got lazy and lost ground I had gained toward my goal:

When I find myself back at "square one," do I give up or start over? How am I using my time in either case? Which choice makes better use of the time I've already spent?

16

No one values time. They give it freely, as though it cost nothing. No one will give you back your years, no one will restore them to you again.

—Seneca, *On the Shortness of Life*, VIII

REFLECT

While frugality is useful and a good practice, have I been trying to DIY things that I could delegate to someone else or pay someone to take care of for me? Am I spending time on these things as though time were infinite and free?

If I valued my time far above my money, what *time-saving* investments would be worth the cost?

17

Remember how long you have been putting things off, and how often you have received an opportunity from the gods, and yet do not use it. You must now at last perceive that a limit of time is fixed for you, which if you do not use it for clearing away the clouds from your mind, it will go and you will go, and it will never return.

—The *Meditations* of Marcus Aurelius,
Book II: iv

REFLECT

A time when I lost an opportunity through my own hesitation or delay, and never got it back:

____

____

____

____

____

____

____

Examples of how I procrastinate or put off doing something important by keeping myself busy with less-important activities:

____

____

____

____

____

____

____

18

When you have remitted your attention for a short time, do not imagine that you will recover it when you choose; but let this thought be present to you—that as a consequence of the fault committed today, your affairs must be in a worse condition for all that follows.

For first, and what causes most trouble, a habit of distraction is formed in you; then a habit of procrastination. And you continually drive away, by deferring it, the happiness of life, proper behavior, and living conformably to nature.

—Epictetus, *The Discourses*, "On Attention"

REFLECT

Things that I put off by telling myself, "It will be better to do it tomorrow / next week / some other time / later":

____

____

____

A time when I felt like procrastinating, but managed to overcome that feeling and just get it done:

____

____

____

____

How I felt afterward:

____

____

____

____

19

Do the external things which fall upon you distract you? Give yourself time to learn something new and good, and cease to be whirled around.

—The *Meditations* of Marcus Aurelius,
Book II: vii

REFLECT

My primary sources of distraction each week:

Three things I could start doing to eliminate these distractions, *one* of which I will begin doing immediately:

20

Postponement is the greatest waste of life.

—Seneca, *On the Shortness of Life*, IX

REFLECT

If I put something off, *why* do I make that choice? What am I actually choosing *instead* of doing what I need to do or what will benefit me in the long run?

How am I *wasting my life* in the ways that I procrastinate?

MY DREAM WEEK

Now imagine a typical week in which you spent every day *fully living*. Write out your schedule for the week spent fully alive, making the best use of your time:

TIME	MONDAY	TUESDAY	WEDNESDAY	THURSDAY	FRIDAY	SATURDAY
12:00 AM						
1:00 AM						
2:00 AM						
3:00AM						
4:00 AM						
5:00 AM						
6:00 AM						
7:00 AM						
9:00 AM						
10:00 AM						
11:00 AM						
12:00 PM						
1:00 PM						
2:00 PM						
3:00 PM						
4:00 PM						
5:00 PM						
6:00 PM						
7:00 PM						
9:00 PM						
10:00 PM						
11:00 PM						

How can I begin to merge this Dream Week Schedule into my real week's schedule? What do I need to remove from my real week to make room?

____

____

____

____

____

____

____

List the Dream Week items that currently can't fit on your real weekly schedule. What would it take to make this possible? Are there short-term steps you can take that will lead to more room for this fully used life?

____

____

____

____

____

____

____

DISCIPLINE

KEY AREAS OF A DISCIPLINED LIFESTYLE

Check off the boxes for the areas where you already have a habit of good discipline:

Health and Fitness:

- ☐ regular exercise
- ☐ consistent sleep schedules
- ☐ nutritious eating habits

Time Management:

- ☐ setting daily goals
- ☐ prioritizing tasks
- ☐ following routines

Financial Discipline:

- ☐ budgeting
- ☐ tracking expenses
- ☐ planning for long-term financial health

Mental & Emotional Discipline:

- ☐ managing stress
- ☐ time spent in healthy emotional relationships
- ☐ expanding your mindset

Digital & Environmental Habits:

- ☐ limiting distractions
- ☐ holding yourself to a limited amount of "screen time"
- ☐ maintaining a clean, organized space

Personal Growth:

- ☐ reading
- ☐ learning new skills
- ☐ developing self-awareness

REFLECT

In which area do you need the most work? Which is your strongest area?

____

____

Which would be the easiest checkbox to work on? Which would be the hardest to improve in?

____

____

Why do you think you have more success in one area than in another? What is it about these types of discipline that makes them easier or harder for you?

____

____

____

____

____

____

21

If you would not have a man flinch when the crisis comes, train him before it comes.

—Seneca, *Letter XVIII*:
"On Festivals and Fasting"

REFLECT

A time when I maintained my discipline in an area well, and it paid off when I faced a bigger challenge:

A big challenge in an area I'm not currently disciplined in and prepared for:

22

When you have said, "Tomorrow I will begin to attend," you must be told that you are saying this, "Today I will be shameless, disregardful of time and place, mean; it will be in the power of others to give me pain; today I will be passionate and envious." See how many evil things you are permitting yourself to do. If it is good to use attention tomorrow, how much better is it to do so today? If tomorrow it is in your interest to attend, much more is it today, that you may be able to do so tomorrow also, and may not defer it again to the third day.

—Epictetus, *The Discourses*,
"On Attention"

REFLECT

Why do I sometimes permit myself to put things off?

How does this quote from Epictetus shift my perspective on procrastination?

23

Nothing great is produced suddenly, since not even the grape or the fig is. If you say to me now that you want a fig, I will answer to you that it requires time. Let it flower first, then put forth fruit, and then ripen. If then the fruit of a fig tree is not perfected suddenly and in one hour, would you possess the fruit of a person's mind in so short a time and so easily?

—Epictetus, *The Discourses*,
"What Philosophy Promises"

REFLECT

A time when I gave up on something because it seemed to be taking too long:

A list of some of the "baby steps" along the way to my current goals:

24

If a thing is difficult to be accomplished by yourself, do not think that it is impossible for a human. But if anything is possible for a human being and conformable to their nature, think that this can be attained by yourself too.

—The *Meditations* of Marcus Aurelius,
Book VI: xix

REFLECT

Something that feels like an impossible task to me:

Someone else who has accomplished it:

Why do I think that this task is possible for them but not for me?

25

The archer must know what he is seeking to hit; then he must aim and control the weapon by his skill. Our plans miscarry because they have no aim. When a man does not know what harbor he is making for, no wind is the right wind.

—Seneca, *Letter LXXI*:
"On the Supreme Good"

REFLECT

Let's find the target! Mental or emotional disturbances I struggle with:

- ☐ worry
- ☐ guilt
- ☐ irritability/anger
- ☐ mood swings
- ☐ sadness
- ☐ isolation
- ☐ unexplained aches, pains, digestive issues
- ☐ constant exhaustion
- ☐ inability to sleep
- ☐ difficulty concentrating
- ☐ racing thoughts
- ☐ memory issues
- ☐ social media addiction
- ☐ binging (food or entertainment)
- ☐ impulsiveness
- ☐ other: ______________________________

My triggers for these problems:

26

The strongest part of the body is that which is exercised by the most frequent use...so by endurance the mind becomes able to despise the power of misfortunes.

—Seneca, *Dialogues*,
"Of Providence," IV

REFLECT

From yesterday's reflection, my areas of weak mental and emotional discipline are:

____

____

____

____

____

____

If I had a physical trainer coaching me through a muscle-building program, they would give me measurable goals to mark my progress. What are some ways of similarly measuring my progress in mental or emotional strength? That is, how would I *know* I was improving in this area, even if I wasn't "there" yet?

____

____

____

____

____

____

27

Philosophers admonish us not to be satisfied with learning only, but also to add study, and then practice. For we have long been accustomed to do contrary things, and we put in practice opinions which are contrary to true opinions. If then we shall not also put in practice right opinions, we shall be nothing more than the expositors of the opinions of others.

—Epictetus, *The Discourses*,
"The Character of a Philosopher"

REFLECT

Areas where my actions don't always reflect the values I claim to agree with:

____

____

____

____

____

____

____

Something I would like to be able to honestly say about myself in the area of mental and emotional discipline:

____

____

____

____

____

____

____

____

28

Neither in writing nor in reading will you be able to lay down rules for others before you shall have first learned to obey rules yourself.

—The *Meditations* of Marcus Aurelius, Book XI: xxix

REFLECT

Areas where I have high standards for the behavior of others:

____

____

____

____

____

____

____

____

Times when I have not been 100% perfect in those areas:

____

____

____

____

____

____

____

____

29

And do you know why we do not have the power to attain this Stoic ideal? It is because we refuse to believe in our power. Nay, of a surety, there is something else which plays a part: it is because we are in love with our vices; we uphold them and prefer to make excuses for them rather than shake them off. We mortals have been endowed with sufficient strength by nature, if only we use this strength, if only we concentrate our powers and rouse them all to help us or at least not to hinder us. The reason is unwillingness, the excuse, inability.

—Seneca, *Letter CXVI*:
"On Self-Control"

REFLECT

So far, why have I struggled to improve in my discipline? Is it because I simply prefer to be the way that I am? Or is it because I am convinced that improving is beyond my ability, so I give up too easily?

____

____

____

One area of discipline from my checklist that I want to improve in:

____

My first measurable "baby step" to getting there:

____

My primary barrier to progress (circle one):

"I can't" **"I don't really want to"**

30

Nothing can be done properly by one who is occupied with something else.

—Seneca, *On the Shortness of Life*, VII

REFLECT

What is distracting me the most from making progress in the area where I need the most discipline?

"I WILL."

From your Disciplined Lifestyle checklist, take three of your weakest areas that you want to improve in:

____

____

____

For each one, write your measurable first baby step—how you will know you have improved (responding differently to one of your triggers, taking action within a time frame, etc.):

____

____

____

Identify for each one whether your barrier is "I can't" or "I don't really want to."

____

____

____

Now you're going to write a statement for each one. Begin with either "I can" or "I really do want to" followed by your first measurable baby step. Then write "because I *will*" and write out your major area that you are going to improve your discipline in.

Example: "I *can* wake up without hitting snooze because I *will* have a consistent schedule and no longer struggle with running late."

My statements for progress:

1. ______________________________

____

____

____

2. ______________________________

____

____

____

3. ______________________________

____

____

____

WISDOM

MY STOIC IDEAL

Describe your ideal Stoic life. What do you hope to gain, personally, from your studies of Stoic teaching?

REFLECT

Things I've learned, whether through experience or direct teaching, that I find have been unhelpful or misguided:

How a Stoic outlook is helping me re-train these lessons into a new personal philosophy and lifestyle:

31

Consider how much more pain is brought on us by the anger and vexation caused by such acts than by the acts themselves, at which we are angry and vexed.

—The *Meditations* of Marcus Aurelius,
Book XI: xviii

REFLECT

A situation that upset me recently:

How much actual physical damage resulted from that situation (to my finances, property, ability to continue living, etc.)?

What consequences did I experience from my *stress* over that situation?

32

When I see a man anxious, I say, "What does this man want?" If he did not want something which is not in his power, how could he be anxious? For this reason a lute player when he is singing by himself has no anxiety, but when he enters the theatre, he is anxious, even if he has a good voice and plays well on the lute; for he not only wishes to sing well, but also to obtain applause—but this is not in his power. Accordingly, where he has skill, there he has confidence.

—Epictetus, *The Discourses*,
"On Anxiety"

REFLECT

In my own life, where do I experience something similar to the example of the lute player? Where do I see myself becoming anxious?

How is my anxiety linked to a desire for something that is not in my power?

33

It is a ridiculous thing for a man not to fly from his own badness, which is indeed possible, but to fly from other men's badness, which is impossible.

—The *Meditations* of Marcus Aurelius,
Book VII: lxxi

REFLECT

What "badness" in other people bothers me most?

Have I ever been guilty of the same thing? Did I react differently when it was my own fault?

34

If any person was intending to put your body in the power of any person whom you fell in with on the way, you would be vexed; but that you put your understanding in the power of any person whom you meet—so that if they should revile you, you are disturbed and troubled—are you not ashamed at this?

—Epictetus, *The Enchiridion*, XXVIII

REFLECT

Do I worry too much about the opinions of others?

Epictetus describes fear of others' opinions with the analogy of being kidnapped and imprisoned. How insightful does this feel to me?

35

No wall can be erected against Fortune which she cannot take by storm; let us strengthen our inner defenses. If the inner part be safe, man can be attacked, but never captured.

—Seneca, *Letter LXXIV*: "On Virtue as a Refuge from Worldly Distractions"

REFLECT

How much time or thought do I spend trying to safeguard against "the whims of fortune" (i.e., sudden health crises or injury, natural disasters, job loss, bereavement, etc.)? What measures do I take for this?

How much time or thought do I put into making myself a stronger person who can face such problems and get through them? How do I measure my inner security against future calamity?

36

If I have set my admiration on the poor body, I have given myself up to be a slave; if on my poor possessions, I also make myself a slave. For I immediately make it plain with what I may be caught.

—Epictetus, *The Discourses*, "How We Should Struggle with Circumstances, II"

REFLECT

What am I a "slave" to? That is, what upsets me most when something happens to it? My health? Finances? Family? Plans? Is this thing within my control or not within my control?

Out of the things that *are* within my control, what appeals to me most? What do I admire most? How can I work to shift my focus away from being a "slave" to something outside of my control, and instead caring more about this thing that *is* within my control?

37

Remember that in life you ought to behave as at a banquet. Suppose that something is carried round and is opposite to you. Stretch out your hand and take a portion with decency. Suppose that it passes by you. Do not detain it. Suppose that it is not yet come to you. Do not send your desire forward to it, but wait till it is opposite to you. Do so with respect to children, so with respect to a wife, so with respect to magisterial offices, so with respect to wealth, and you will someday be a worthy partner of the banquets of the gods.

—Epictetus, *The Enchiridion*, XV

REFLECT

What things in life do I spent the most time desiring and impatiently waiting for? What things do I have the hardest time letting go of, when it's time?

Rather than those things, what do I have "in front of me at the table" right now? How can I focus more on the things that are currently being given to me to do and experience?

38

Nothing is more wretched than a person who seeks by conjecture what is in the minds of their neighbors, without perceiving that it is sufficient to attend to their own spirit within, and to reverence it sincerely. And reverence of the spirit consists in keeping it pure from passion and thoughtlessness and dissatisfaction.

—The *Meditations* of Marcus Aurelius,
Book II: xiii

REFLECT

Everyone has times when they worry about what someone else is thinking of them. When have I done this, and come up with my own guesses about what someone else thought, but eventually I discovered that I was totally wrong?

____

____

____

____

____

What did this experience teach me about using all that time an energy to figure out what other people think? And in general, whose minds do I still "reverence" above my own? Whose opinions matter more to me that my own?

____

____

____

____

____

____

39

Appearances to the mind are of four kinds. Things either are what they appear to be; or they neither are, nor appear to be; or they are, and do not appear to be; or they are not, and yet appear to be. Rightly to aim in all these cases is the wise man's task.

—Epictetus, *The Discourses*, "Appearances and What Aids We Should Provide Against Them"

REFLECT

Things that are (truths), but which don't appear real or true to me:

____

____

____

Things that are not true or real, but I react as though they were:

____

____

____

How could I better respond to these things, knowing that they are deceptive appearances?

____

____

____

____

40

Be not disgusted, nor discouraged, nor dissatisfied, if you do not succeed in doing everything according to right principles, but when you have failed, return back again, and be content if the greater part of what you do is consistent with human nature, and love this to which you return.

—The *Meditations* of Marcus Aurelius,
Book V: ix

REFLECT

How am I doing so far on this Stoic journey? Have I made a lot of progress? Am I disappointed in my lack of progress?

Where have I failed most, so far? Have I been brave enough to try again? Or have I avoided or given up in that area?

MY STOIC JOURNEY

Going back to your description of your ideal Stoic life, fill in this chart:

Where I have made progress so far:
Where I still have a long way to go:
Where I have failed and given up:
Where I have failed and tried again:

REFLECT

My Stoic Journey is about the active application in your life. Now let's look at things that you may not have taken action on yet, but which are "food for thought."

How Stoic teaching is helping me re-frame my thinking, and what new perspectives on my life I have been gaining so far:

JUSTICE

Injustices in the world or society that bother me most:

41

How much trouble you avoid if you do not look to see what your neighbor says or does or thinks, but only to what you do yourself, that it may be just and pure. Look not round at the depraved morals of others, but run straight along the line without deviating from it.

—The *Meditations* of Marcus Aurelius,
Book IV: xviii

REFLECT

One time when I did not do something that I thought was right (or did do something that I thought was wrong) because of what other people thought:

One time when I acted rightly, no matter what anyone thought:

42

When you have decided that a thing ought to be done, and are doing it, never avoid being seen doing it, though the many shall form an unfavorable opinion about it. For if it is not right to do it, avoid doing the thing; but if it is right, why are you afraid of those who shall find fault wrongly?

—Epictetus, *The Enchiridion*, XXXV

REFLECT

One time when I did the right thing but tried to keep people from finding out about it (and why):

How hard is it for me to do the right thing (or not do the wrong thing) when it goes against what others expect? Why?

43

He who does not prevent a crime, when he can, encourages it.

—Seneca, *Troades* (The Trojan Women)

REFLECT

Have I ever failed to step up and stop something from happening that I knew wasn't right?

How would I handle that differently if I could go back and do it again?

44

The best way of avenging yourself is to not become like the wrongdoer.

—The *Meditations* of Marcus Aurelius,
Book VI: vi

REFLECT

Have I experienced a time when someone treated me badly, and it left such an impression on me that I resolved never to be like that? Have I lived up to that choice?

____

____

____

____

____

____

Looking back at my list of injustices at the beginning of this section, what do I do to actively keep myself from participating in any of these?

____

____

____

____

____

____

____

45

We are prone to believe many things which we are willing to hear, and so we conclude, and take up a prejudice before we can judge. Never condemn a friend unheard; or without letting him know his accuser, or his crime.

—Seneca, *De Ira* (On Anger):
Book 10.

REFLECT

Is it easier to believe gossip about a friend or a stranger? Am I prone to share gossip about one, but not the other?

How might gossip or rumor-mongering in themselves be considered an injustice?

46

Kindly remember that he whom you call your slave sprang from the same stock, is smiled upon by the same skies, and on equal terms with yourself breathes, lives, and dies.

—Seneca, *Letter XLVII*:
"On Master and Slave"

REFLECT

How do I treat those under me—whether they are subordinates at work, my own children, or simply an HVAC technician I've hired or a waitress bringing my food? Do I ever stop and think that this person is a human just like me?

As a member of the human race, what can I do to remind myself that all people are human just like me? How should this inform my treatment of them?

47

We ought to accommodate ourselves to the ignorant and to say: "This person recommends to me that which he thinks good for himself. I excuse him."

—Epictetus, *The Discourses*, "On Constancy"

REFLECT

When someone tries to give me bad advice, not knowing their mistake, how do I react? Do I look down on them? Do I try to correct them, even if they can't understand my correction?

When I meet someone who holds to opinions and values I consider totally wrong, how successful am I at remembering this person is an equal in the human family with me? What do I tend to do instead, to distance myself from them or put them in a separate (possibly inferior) category?

48

To be angry with a man is to hate him; to hate him is to wish him harm; but to wish him well, even if he has done you harm, is the mark of a great mind.

—Seneca, *De Ira* (On Anger): Book 2

REFLECT

People who have harmed me, and what they did:

How I responded to those wounds:

Have I ever been successful at wishing any of these people well?

49

O slavish man! will you not bear with your own brother, who has God for his Father, as being a son from the same stock, and of the same high descent? But if you chance to be placed in some superior station, will you presently set yourself up for a tyrant?

—Epictetus, *The Discourses*, "How Everything May Be Done Acceptably"

REFLECT

If I were made ruler of the world, what would I change? What good would I choose to do?

How might my "good laws" look like tyranny to people who are different from me?

50

You can pass your life in an equable flow of happiness if you can go by the right way, and think and act in the right way.

—The *Meditations* of Marcus Aurelius,
Book V: xxxiv

REFLECT

As far as I am able (my actions, which are within my own control), do I do what I consider right? It is ever difficult? Why?

Which is more difficult—to do what I think is right, or to allow other people to do what they think is right, even if I think it is wrong (not counting actual crimes)? Do I try to control the actions of others when it comes to my sense of correct behavior?

Revisiting my list of injustices from the beginning of this section:

Society-wide injustice is outside of most people's individual control. But you can control your own actions in a small way and choose to be just. Write a statement for each injustice, making a personal choice not to act unjustly even in the smallest way.

For example: "Racism is an injustice in society, but I will act justly by making sure that I treat everyone I meet as my equal in the human family."

____

____

____

____

____

____

____

____

____

____

____

____

____

____

TEMPERENCE

Areas where self-control and moderation are easy for me (**write in your specific victories**):

Appetite (food, drink, pleasure)

Action (work, accomplishments, hobbies, and entertainment)

Attitude (emotional expressions or outbursts)

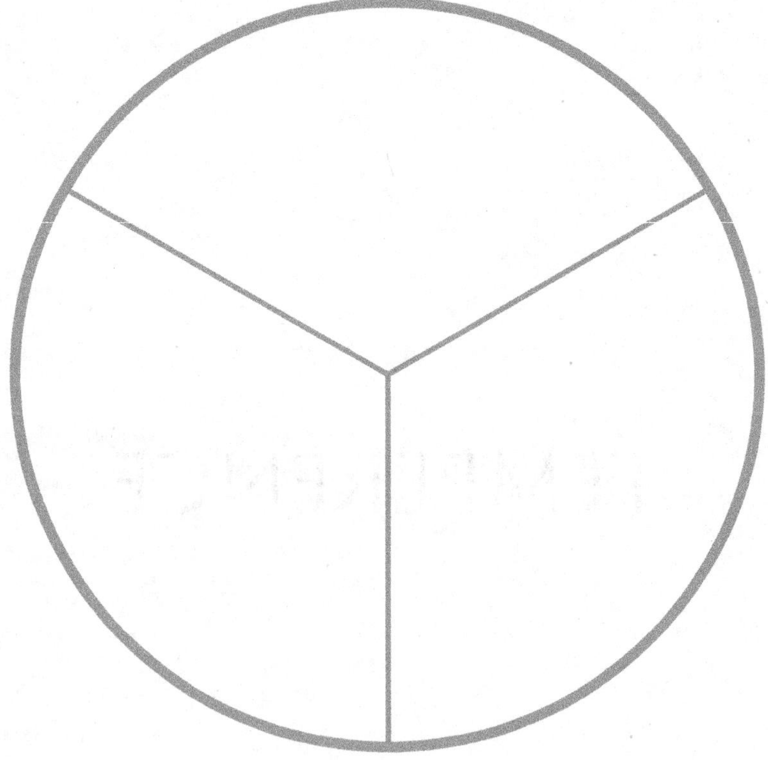

Area where self-control and moderation are a challenge for me or I sometimes lose control (**write in your specific areas of weakness**):

Appetite (food, drink, pleasure)

Action (work, accomplishments, hobbies)

Attitude (emotional expressions or outbursts)

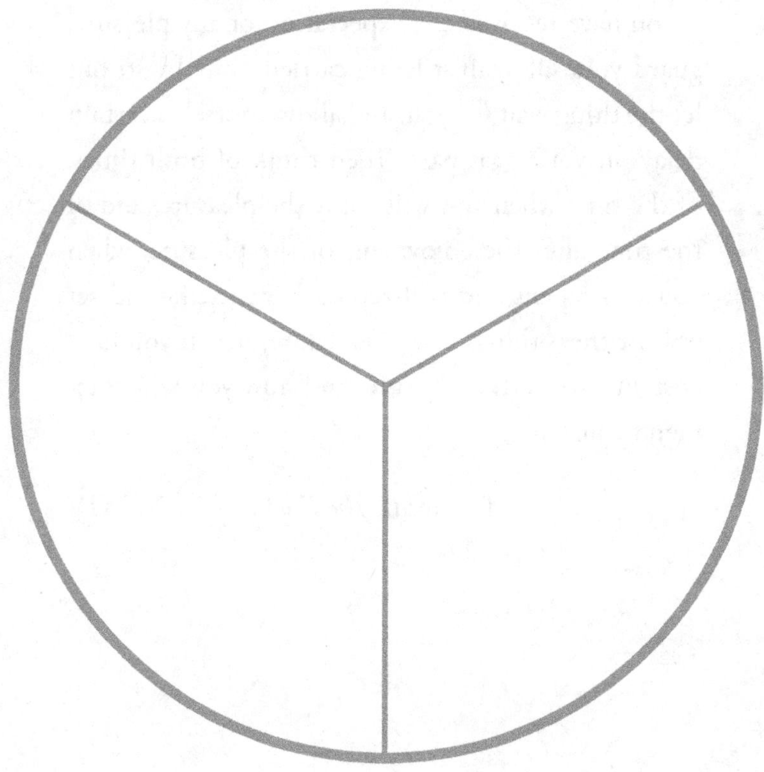

51

If you have received the expectation of any pleasure, guard yourself against being carried away by it; but let the thing wait for you, and allow yourself a certain delay on your own part. Then think of both times, of the time when you will enjoy the pleasure, and of the time after the enjoyment of the pleasure, when you will repent and will reproach yourself. And set against these things how you will rejoice, if you have abstained from the pleasure, and how you will commend yourself.

—Epictetus, *The Enchiridion*, XXXIV

REFLECT

Times I have felt guilty or disappointed in myself after over-indulgence:

- ____________________
- ____________________
- ____________________
- ____________________
- ____________________
- ____________________
- ____________________
- ____________________
- ____________________
- ____________________
- ____________________
- ____________________
- ____________________
- ____________________
- ____________________
- ____________________
- ____________________
- ____________________
- ____________________

52

Let the part of your soul which leads and governs be undisturbed by the movements in the flesh, whether of pleasure or of pain; and let it not unite with them, but let it circumscribe itself and limit those affects to their parts.

—The *Meditations* of Marcus Aurelius,
Book V: xxvi

REFLECT

Some of the most intense experiences of pleasure and pain in my life have been:

When I'm experiencing pleasure or pain, am I able to keep a part of myself in reserve from the experience? Or do I have a tendency to be swept up and unaware of any part of myself outside of the pleasure or pain?

53

It is a mark of a mean capacity to spend much time on the things which concern the body, such as much exercise, much eating, much drinking, much easing of the body, much copulation. But these things should be done as subordinate things; and let all your care be directed to the mind.

—Epictetus, *The Enchiridion*, XLI

REFLECT

If I separate my mind from any part of my physical existence, how would I describe myself? Do I spend more time as this person, or am I usually identifying myself with my physical experiences?

____

____

____

____

____

Which do I spend more time taking care of—my mind or my body? If I do nothing else but feed my body, I still do that two or three times every day. What do I do every day to take care of my mind?

____

____

____

____

____

____

54

How many pleasures have been enjoyed by robbers, patricides, tyrants!

—The *Meditations* of Marcus Aurelius,
Book VI: xxxiv

REFLECT

My favorite thing to do:

If a famously horrible person also liked my favorite activity, would that change my feelings about it? If so, am I too attached to my pleasures?

How could I develop a healthy, moderate enjoyment of everything I like, without focusing too much on these things?

55

Be not hurried away by excitement, but say, "Appearances, wait for me a little; let me see who you are, and what you are about; let me put you to the test." And then bring in to oppose it some other beautiful and noble appearance, and cast out this base appearance.

—Epictetus, *The Discourses*, "How We Should Struggle Against Appearances"

REFLECT

Are there things I enjoy to excess because I get swept up in their superficial attractions?

____

____

____

____

____

____

Can I find something that is more inherently good and valuable in comparison to the things that strain my self-control? How can I shift my focus to better things and thus improve my temperance?

____

____

____

____

____

____

____

56

Wipe out the imagination; check desire; extinguish appetite; keep the ruling faculty in its own power. Stop the pulling of the strings. Confine yourself to the present. Let the wrong which is done by a person stay there where the wrong was done.

—The *Meditations* of Marcus Aurelius,
Book VII: xxix; IX: vii

REFLECT

When I'm struggling with self-control, am I looking toward the future, dwelling too much in the past, or am I caught up in the moment without a thought for consequences?

When my reason tells me to restrain myself, why do I ignore it?

57

In company take care not to speak much and excessively about your own acts or accomplishments; for as it is pleasant to you to make mention of your own accomplishments, it is not so pleasant to others to hear what has happened to you.

—Epictetus, *The Enchiridion*, XXXIII

REFLECT

How is self-control in the area of what I say also a temperance issue? Have I ever looked at it that way before? Do I lack self-control in my speech?

Temperence is also about being sensitive to the preferences of others—not inflicting my likes and dislikes on people simply because I lack awareness and self-control. Would others say that I practice temperance in this area well, or would they point out some problems?

58

The cause of anger is the belief that we are injured; this belief, therefore, should not be lightly entertained. We ought not to fly into a rage even when the injury appears to be open and distinct: for some false things bear the semblance of truth. We should always allow some time to elapse, for time discloses the truth.

—Seneca, *De Ira* (On Anger): Book 2

REFLECT

Anger is often one of the hardest emotions to control. How do I manage my anger when someone upsets me? Am I one who has obvious outbursts, or do I use some other coping mechanism to process my anger? Could this be related to any of the areas of temperance that I struggle in?

____

____

____

____

____

Seeking the truth and choosing not to believe I am injured are rational responses that assist my self-control against anger. What other rational responses can I use to combat my struggles in temperance?

____

____

____

____

____

59

If you have assumed a character above your strength, you have both acted in an unbecoming way, and you have neglected that which you might have fulfilled.

—Epictetus, *The Enchiridion*, XXXVII

REFLECT

How temperate is my own opinion of myself? Are there times I over- or under-estimate my own abilities?

One time when I thought I could handle more than I really could:

How that situation might have gone differently if my self-assessment had been temperate and I had been able to focus on doing what was actually within my power:

60

Bear with the person who is unlike yourself. Be kind to him, gentle, ready to pardon on account of his ignorance, on account of his being mistaken in things of the greatest importance. Be harsh to no one, being well convinced of Plato's doctrine that every mind is deprived of truth unwillingly.

—Epictetus, *The Discourses*, "On Friendship"

REFLECT

Is it more of a struggle for me to be self-controlled in my own lifestyle, or in my interactions with others?

People who spring to mind as being those to whom I struggle to be kind:

What mistaken beliefs are they operating under? How can I use my understanding of this to strengthen my self-control toward them?

As I've been looking over the idea of temperance, or self-control, in this past section, what new items might I need to add to my struggles?

Successes?

VIRTUE

AN IDEAL PERSON

Write a description of someone you would consider a really good person. What makes them good? How do they act? What is or isn't a part of their life or personality?

REFLECT

Why do these particular attributes stand out to me as being an important part of a good person?

____

____

____

____

____

____

____

What types of virtue am I most focused on—active or passive, behavior or emotion?

____

____

____

____

____

____

____

____

61

If it is not right, do not do it; if it is not true, do not say it.

—The *Meditations* of Marcus Aurelius,
Book XII: xvii

REFLECT

Do I struggle with telling the truth? Under what circumstances do I use half-truths or white lies?

How important do I think 100% honesty is to a virtuous life? Was this a part of my description of the ideal person? Why or why not?

62

Men do not care how nobly they live, but only how long, although it is within the reach of every man to live nobly, but within no man's power to live long.

—Seneca, *Letter XXII*:
"On the Futility of Half-Way Measures"

REFLECT

How much do I want to live a virtuous life? How does it compare to the way I feel about not dying young?

What would I do if I had the option of a short but virtuous life or a long but morally corrupt one?

63

No longer talk at all about the kind of person that a good person ought to be, but be such.

—The *Meditations* of Marcus Aurelius,
Book X: xvi

REFLECT

Times when I've planned to change but failed in the execution:

How valid are those goals? Were they unreasonable, or were they good goals and I need to try again? How much would even a small success help me?

64

What is the first business of one who practices philosophy? To get rid of self-conceit. For it is impossible for anyone to begin to learn that which he thinks he already knows.

—Epictetus, *The Discourses*, "How We Must Adapt Preconceptions to Particular Cases"

REFLECT

A time when I discovered that I didn't actually know something, although I thought I did:

How can I prevent future reoccurrences of this? Since I don't currently know the things I'm unaware of, how can I find out before my ignorance leads me into error?

65

If one should suddenly ask, "What have you now in your thoughts?" with perfect openness you should be able to immediately answer, "This or that." From your words it should be plain that everything in you is simple and benevolent.

—The *Meditations* of Marcus Aurelius,
Book III: iv

REFLECT

Times when I have been asked something and had to pause and weigh my answer:

When I finally answered, how truthful was I? If I wasn't 100% honest, what was holding me back?

66

We often want one thing and pray for another, not telling the truth even to the gods.

—Seneca, *Letter XCV*:
"On the Usefulness of Basic Principles"

REFLECT

Do I lie to my own soul? Can I think of any occasions when I've tried to sugar-coat my own desires, plans, or motives to make myself feel better about my choices?

How would perfect honesty with myself help me become more virtuous in my outward life?

67

Never value anything as profitable which will compel you to break your promise, to lose your self-respect, to hate anyone, to suspect, to curse, to act the hypocrite, to desire anything which needs walls and curtains.

—The *Meditations* of Marcus Aurelius,
Book III: vii

REFLECT

What's my price? What would someone have to give me in order for me to do something I consider wrong?

Whatever that "price" is, why do I value it enough to exchange my own goodness for it?

68

In walking about, as you take care not to step on a nail, or to sprain your foot, so take care not to damage your own ruling faculty [soul]; and if we observe this rule in every act, we shall undertake this act with more security.

—Epictetus, *The Enchiridion*, XXXVIII

REFLECT

Do I protect my own moral integrity with this level of caution? If I were driving in a snow storm, I would be careful so that I don't get into an accident and get hurt or wreck my car. How careful am I about my soul as I go through my day?

What can I do to make myself more aware of the perils of daily life that threaten to cause injury to my mind and soul?

69

The happy man is he whose possessions are all in his soul, who is upright and exalted, who spurns inconstancy, who sees no man with whom he wishes to change places, who rates men only at their value as men, who takes Nature for his teacher, conforming to her laws and living as she commands, whom no violence can deprive of his possessions, who turns evil into good, is unerring in judgment, unshaken, unafraid, who may be moved by force but never moved to distraction.

—Seneca, *Letter XLV*:
"On Sophistical Argumentation"

REFLECT

Who would I trade lives with? Why?

What would it take to be able to say, "No, I wouldn't trade places with them. I'm better off being me"?

70

Now if virtue promises good fortune and tranquility and happiness, certainly also the progress toward virtue is progress toward each of these things. For it is always true that to whatever point the perfecting of anything leads us, progress is an approach toward this point.

—Epictetus, *The Discourses*,
"Of Progress or Improvement"

REFLECT

What is the point of virtue, for me? Happiness? Good fortune? Tranquility? How does a virtuous life get me there?

How can I measure my progress in this area?

A NEW IDEAL

Describe your ideal version of yourself. Take into consideration the reflections on different aspects of virtue from this section. What is new to this ideal? What has changed?

How much does my ability to live virtuously depend on factors that are not within my control (i.e., other people's behavior, external circumstances, money, etc.)?

NATURE

The aspects of my life and my identity that have been given to me by Nature, and which I have accepted and am content with:

- ____
- ____
- ____
- ____
- ____
- ____
- ____
- ____

The aspects of my life and my identity, given by Nature, which I cannot accept, which I have tried to change, or which I struggle to be happy with:

- ____
- ____
- ____
- ____
- ____
- ____
- ____
- ____

71

Nothing is evil which is according to nature.

—*The Meditations of Marcus Aurelius,*
Book II: xvii

REFLECT

Do I struggle to agree with this quote? Are there things that happen naturally that I feel are evil?

What about death? Is death natural, or is it evil? How so?

72

Whatever happens, assume that it was bound to happen, and do not be willing to rail at Nature. That which you cannot reform, it is best to endure.

—Seneca, Letter CVII:
On Obedience to the Universal Will

REFLECT

Can I apply this philosophy to all those things that are outside of my control? How?

What should I do if it seems to me that things outside of my control are happening in a way that is not natural? Is there a way for me to accept them, or is this where I depart from Stoic philosophy?

73

Observe constantly that all things take place by change, and accustom yourself to consider that the nature of the universe loves nothing so much as to change the things which are and to make new things like them. For everything that exists is in a manner the seed of that which will be.

—The *Meditations* of Marcus Aurelius,
Book IV: xxxvi

REFLECT

Some of the natural cycles of change I have experienced in my life:

Am I facing any potential upcoming changes that are also part of the natural cycle? How do I feel about approaching change? How well do I embrace it as part of Nature?

74

What you love is nothing of your own; it has been given to you for the present, not that it should not be taken from you, nor has it been given to you for all time, but as a fig is given to you or a bunch of grapes at the appointed season of the year. But if you wish for these things in winter, you are a fool.

—Epictetus, *The Discourses*,
"That We Ought Not to Be Moved"

REFLECT

Some major seasons in my life when I lost something or gained something new:

In my experiences with natural loss and gain, which do I resist? Which do I eagerly accept? What kinds of pattern can I see here?

75

What does the work of a fig tree is a fig tree, and what does the work of a dog is a dog, and what does the work of a bee is a bee, and what does the work of a human is a human.

—The *Meditations* of Marcus Aurelius,
Book X: viii

REFLECT

How I would describe my role in the universe as a human being:

Do I ever try to take on roles that are not my own? What kinds, and why (if so)?

76

Does the sun undertake to do the work of the rain? And how is it with respect to each of the stars—are they not different and yet they work together to the same end?

—The *Meditations* of Marcus Aurelius,
Book VI: xliii

REFLECT

My favorite aspect of Nature to observe and contemplate is:

The natural cycles I see here, and the parts that all work together, each in their own place, are:

77

Humans are formed by nature to acts of benevolence. When they have done anything benevolent or in any other way conducive to the common interest, they have acted conformably to their constitution, and they get what is their own.

—The *Meditations* of Marcus Aurelius,
Book IX: xlii

REFLECT

Does benevolence feel like an instinctive part of human nature to me—as much as the patterns of Nature that I observe? What observations are informing my feelings about human nature here?

____

____

____

____

____

____

Can I come up with some examples and situations in which humans *do* act with natural selflessness, care, and generosity toward each other?

____

____

____

____

____

____

78

Everything has two handles—the one by which it may be borne, the other by which it may not. If your brother acts unjustly, do not lay hold of the act by that handle wherein he acts unjustly, for this is the handle which cannot be borne; but lay hold of the other, that he is your brother, that he was nurtured with you, and you will lay hold of the thing by that handle by which it can be borne.

—Epictetus, *The Enchiridion*, XLIII

REFLECT

An injustice that I struggle to tolerate is:

If I deepen my understanding of the people involved, focusing on their human nature, which is the same nature I have, how does this affect my feelings toward the human being whose actions I dislike?

79

Anger, as we have said, is eager to punish; and that such a desire should exist in man's peaceful breast is least of all according to his nature; for human life is founded on benefits and harmony and is bound together into an alliance for the common help of all, not by terror, but by love towards one another.

—Seneca, *On Anger to Novatus*

REFLECT

When have I excused or justified my own anger by considering it natural, under the circumstances?

How does the concept that anger is unnatural connect with the Stoic view of the difference between things within my control and things outside of my control?

80

Whosoever is terrible to others is likewise afraid of himself. What is more ordinary than for a tyrant to be destroyed by his own guards? which is no more than the putting those crimes into practice which they learned of their masters. How many slaves have revenged themselves of their cruel oppressors, though they were sure to die for it!

—Seneca, *De Ira* (On Anger): Book 12

REFLECT

In order to treat my fellow human beings with more compassion, do I possibly need to love myself more? How might my impatience with others relate to parts of myself I dislike or struggle to accept?

In what ways might my difficult relationships be showing me how I have become out of tune with Nature and my place in the natural cycle?

ANOTHER LOOK AT NATURE

Going back to your lists from the beginning of this section, what new perspectives have you gained on your place in the universe?

SERENITY

The things in my life that consistently upset me, steal my peace, and disrupt my serenity:

Self-care techniques that I use to find serenity:

Rank these in order of how well they work, and indicate how *long* they work:

81

To nature who gives and takes back all, the one who is instructed and modest says, "Give what you will; take back what you will." And they say this not proudly, but obediently, and well pleased with her.

—The *Meditations* of Marcus Aurelius,
Book X: xiv

REFLECT

What things do I have a hard time letting go of?

Have I ever experienced a loss that I was prepared for and ready to accept? How does this attitude make me more resilient?

82

The wise man is joyful, happy, and calm; unshaken, he lives on a plane with the gods.

—Seneca, *Letter LIX*:
"On Pleasure and Joy"

REFLECT

Taking one item from my list of things that disrupt my serenity, how would it look if I were able to remain calm when that happens?

How does this kind of serenity make me more resilient in my daily life, over the long term?

83

Everything harmonizes with me, which is harmonious to you, O Universe. Nothing for me is too early nor too late, which is in due time for you. Everything is fruit to me which your seasons bring, O Nature: from you are all things, in you are all things, to you all things return.

—The *Meditations* of Marcus Aurelius,
Book IV: xxiii

REFLECT

Where can I make a small, practical beginning in the habit of taking Nature as it comes? (For example: remaining in harmony and serenity despite the changing seasons—even when in the midst of a season whose weather I don't like.)

What joy can I find in these moments that increases my overall serenity?

84

Seek not that the things which happen should happen as you wish; but wish the things which happen to be as they are, and you will have a tranquil flow of life.

—Epictetus, *The Enchiridion*, VIII

REFLECT

In what areas am I still extending my desires beyond things that are within my control? How does that affect my serenity, when things don't happen the way I wanted them to?

Which is more important—my preferences for these events, or my internal serenity?

If everything happened exactly the way I wanted it to and I was never contradicted, would that be a good thing for my character? How resilient would I become, under such conditions?

85

When any person treats you ill or speaks ill of you, remember that they do this or say this because they think that it is their duty. It is not possible then for them to follow that which seems right to you, but that which seems right to themselves. Accordingly, if they are wrong in their opinion, they are the person who is hurt, for they are the person who has been deceived.

—Epictetus, *The Enchiridion*, XLII

REFLECT

A time when someone did something wrong and upset me:

A time when someone made a very foolish mistake and I felt sorry for them:

How can I change my response to the first event by looking upon it with the same perspective as I had in the second event?

86

If you are pained by any external thing, it is not this thing that disturbs you, but your own judgment about it. And it is in your power to wipe out this judgment now.

—The *Meditations* of Marcus Aurelius,
Book VIII: xlvii

REFLECT

My current grievances/sources of emotional or mental pain:

- ____
- ____
- ____
- ____
- ____
- ____
- ____

The opinions I am holding that cause me to be pained by these things:

____

____

____

____

____

____

____

____

____

87

How are you desirous at the same time to live to old age, and at the same time not to see the death of any person whom you love? Know you not that in the course of a long time many and various kinds of things must happen?

—Epictetus, *The Discourses*,
"That We Ought Not to Be Moved"

REFLECT

In what ways have I over-idealized my expectations for life? (Such as in the example of the quote—hoping to live a long time but never lose anyone.)

____

____

____

____

____

____

When I look at this list, how can I re-frame these expectations into more realistic ones, knowing that some things are inevitable? How will these realistic expectations make me more resilient when bad things happen?

____

____

____

____

____

____

88

What is the divine law? To keep a person's own, not to claim that which belongs to others, but to use what is given, and when it is not given, not to desire it; and when a thing is taken away, to give it up readily and immediately, and to be thankful for the time that a person has had the use of it.

—Epictetus, *The Discourses*,
"That We Do Not Strive to Use Our Opinions
About Good and Evil"

REFLECT

Things I have had to give up or things that I have lost in the past, which I am still unhappy about losing:

How can I re-frame my feelings about these things, looking back with gratitude and releasing them as no longer mine?

89

We are all chained to fortune: the chain of one is made of gold, and long, while that of another is short and rusty. But what difference does it make? The same prison surrounds all of us. All life is slavery. Therefore each one must accustom himself to his own condition and complain about it as little as possible, and lay hold of whatever good is to be found near him. Nothing is so bitter that a calm mind cannot find comfort in it. Apply reason to difficulties; harsh circumstances can be softened, narrow limits can be widened, and burdensome things can be made to press less severely on those who bear them cleverly.

—Seneca,
On Tranquility of the Mind

REFLECT

What difficulties and troubles have I been able to overcome by taking a more Stoic and rational view of them?

Which parts of my life still bother me most? Where can I find some small comfort or good thing in these areas, which can help me become more serene in the future?

90

Seek not the good in things external; seek it in yourselves. If you do not, you will not find it.

—Epictetus, *The Discourses*,
"That We Ought Not to Be Moved"

REFLECT

Today, I list all the good things I can find within myself, my mind, my soul, and my character:

MY RESILIENT LIFE

Go back to the list of self-care techniques you used to combat things that disrupt your serenity (at the beginning of this section). Here, replace any temporary "band-aid" techniques with something from your list above—the good things you find within your own soul. How can you focus more on the true good within so that you rely less on external comforts to find your serenity?

THANK YOU FOR READING THIS BOOK!

If you found any of the information helpful, please take a few minutes and leave a review on the bookselling platform of your choice.

BONUS GIFT!

Don't forget to sign up for our newsletter and grab your free personal development ebook here:

soundwisdom.com/classics